JAN 2019

TRAVEL WITH THE GREAT EXPLORERS

Explore with

Ibn Battuta

Rachel Stuckey

Crabtree Publishing Company
www.crabtreebooks.com

Crabtree Publishing Company
www.crabtreebooks.com

Author: Rachel Stuckey

Managing Editor: Tim Cooke

Designer: Lynne Lennon

Picture Manager: Sophie Mortimer

Design Manager: Keith Davis

Editorial Director: Lindsey Lowe

Children's Publisher: Anne O'Daly

Crabtree Editorial Director: Kathy Middleton

Crabtree Editor: Petrice Custance

Proofreader: Angela Kaelberer

**Production coordinator
and prepress technician:** Tammy McGarr

Print coordinator: Margaret Amy Salter

Written and produced for Crabtree Publishing Company
by Brown Bear Books

Photographs:
Front Cover: **Alamy:** Lanmas main; **Shutterstock:** BBH cr;
Thinkstock: istockphoto tr, br.

Interior: **Alamy:** Art Collection 3 20, Dominic Byrne 27bl, Chronicle
21b, Granger Collection 17c, Peter Horree 5r, Indiapicture 19br,
Alan King Engraving 26tr, Lanmas 5t, Ian Masteron 14, Werner
Forman Archive 15b; **Getty Images:** Dean Conger 12b, Izzet Keribar
25bl, NurPhoto 24; **istockphoto:** 22t, 29b; **Library of Congress:** 6;
**Metropolitan Museum
of Art:** Rogers Fund 18; **Public Domain:** asianhistory.com 10tl;
Shutterstock: 19t, 23br, Bariterek Media 13t, Irina Burakova 15t,
Mikhail Dudarev 23, Karol Koziowski 10br, Yongyut Kumsri 4,
Victor Lauer 11, Motion Works Film Studio 7t, Nyvit-art 17br, Taiga 7l,
Mirza Visoko 26bl, Oleg Zhukov 22b; **Thinkstock:** Dorling Kindersley
25r, istockphoto 21t, 27t, Lukasz Nowak 28; **Topfoto:** Fine Art Images/
HIP 29t, Granger Collection 12t, 13b, 16.
All other artwork and maps, **Brown Bear Books Ltd.**

Brown Bear Books has made every attempt to contact the
copyright holder. If you have any information please contact
licensing@brownbearbooks.co.uk

Library and Archives Canada Cataloguing in Publication

CIP Available at the Library and Archives Canada

Library of Congress Cataloging-in-Publication Data

CIP Available at the Library of Congress

Crabtree Publishing Company
www.crabtreebooks.com   1-800-387-7650

Printed in Canada/092017/PB20170719

Published in Canada
Crabtree Publishing
616 Welland Ave.
St. Catharines, ON
L2M 5V6

Published in the United States
Crabtree Publishing
PMB 59051
350 Fifth Avenue, 59th Floor
New York, New York 10118

Published in the United Kingdom
Crabtree Publishing
Maritme House
Basin Road North, Hove
BN41 1WR

Published in Australia
Crabtree Publishing
3 Charles Street
Coburg North
VIC, 3058

CONTENTS

Meet the Boss	4
Where Are We Heading?	6
Ibn Battuta's Travels in Dar al-Islam	8
Meet the Crew	10
Check Out the Ride	12
Solve It With Science	14
Hanging at Home	16
Meeting and Greeting	18
Far From Home	20
I Love Nature	22
Fortune Hunting	24
This Isn't What It Said in the Brochure!	26
End of the Road	28
Glossary & Timeline	30
On the Web & Books	31
Index	32

Meet the Boss

Abu Abdullah Muhammad Ibn Battuta was probably the best-traveled person of the Middle Ages. In 30 years he traveled about 75,000 miles (120,700 kilometers) from Spain in the west to China in the east.

Did you know ?

Ibn Battuta left Tangier at the age of 21. He set out alone and suffered from bad homesickness. He said that he was compelled to leave home by his desire to see the famous sites of Islam in Arabia.

BERBER BACKGROUND

+ Traditional Peoples

Ibn Battuta was born in 1304 in Tangier, Morocco. His family were Berbers. The Berbers were a traditional people who lived throughout North Africa. They mainly followed the **Sunni** branch of **Islam**. Many Berbers still live in Morocco today (above), and their culture is carefully preserved.

IS IT TRUE?

★ An Unreliable Account

★ Did Ibn Battuta Fib?

Ibn Battuta did not keep a journal or diary. After he returned home from 30 years of traveling, his account was written in a book entitled *Rihla*, or *Travels*. Modern experts say that some dates and details in the book are wrong. Some passages even come from the work of other writers. It is likely Ibn Battuta could not accurately remember all his 30 years of traveling. This makes the *Rihla* unreliable as a source of history. However, scholars agree the story is generally true. It also provides many details about life in the Islamic world at the time.

Ibn Battuta's father was a *qadi*, or a judge of Islamic **sharia** law. Ibn Battuta also studied Islamic law and became a qadi. When he traveled throughout the Islamic world, Ibn Battuta reported that he was welcomed in many places, partly because of his useful legal knowledge. He also learned some of the languages of the places he visited, such as Persian, so he could communicate more easily.

HEADING TO MECCA

+ Going on Pilgrimage

In 628, the Prophet Muhammad traveled to Mecca in Arabia with his 1,400 followers. Later, it became the duty of all Muslims to make a **pilgrimage** to Mecca (right) if they could. This pilgrimage, or *hajj*, is an expression of devotion to God. Pilgrims purify themselves, wear simple clothes, and perform acts of worship together. Ibn Battuta's first journey began in 1325 when he made his first hajj. He then decided to explore the rest of the Muslim world.

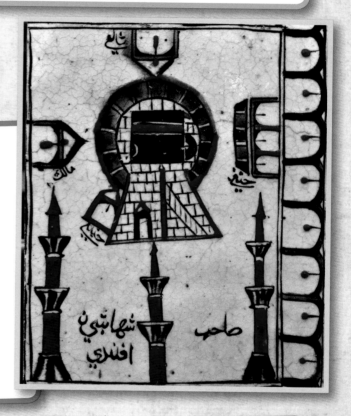

WIVES AND CHILDREN

★ Marries many times

Ibn Battuta married at least 10 times on his travels and had at least five children. Islamic law allowed men to be married to more than one woman at a time. Women had very little freedom at the time. They were expected to stay at home and care for their families. Ibn Battuta left his families behind when he traveled to a new place. He often divorced his wives.

Where Are We Heading?

In Ibn Battuta's time, southern Spain, North Africa, the Middle East, and Central Asia were all Muslim regions. Much of southern Asia also had large Muslim populations.

Did you know ?

Since its founding in the 600s, Islam had spread widely. Virtually all of Ibn Battuta's travels took place in Islamic countries. The Islamic world was known as Dar al-Islam.

CENTER OF TRADE

- ☞ Tabriz is on the Silk Road
- ☞ Meeting place for merchants

In the 1200s, the Mongols set up a huge empire in Central Asia. They made Tabriz (above), in modern-day Iranian Azerbaijan, an important center on the Silk Road. This long trade route joined East and South Asia to Europe, via Anatolia. In 1327, Ibn Battuta briefly visited Tabriz. He said it was home to many merchants from Europe and China.

TRAVEL UPDATE

Get a Job!

★ On a long journey, raise money by working along the way. In 1334, when Ibn Battuta reached India, he got a job with the **sultan**. Ibn Battuta spent six years traveling through India as a judge. Eventually the sultan selected Ibn Battua to act as his **ambassador** in China.

- ☞ Tropical islands
- ☞ A new master

The Maldives are 26 islands spread out in the Indian Ocean. Ibn Battuta stopped there on his way from India to China. The Maldives had been a Buddhist nation, but it had recently converted to Islam and needed an expert in Islamic law. The sultan of the Maldives made Ibn Battuta stay and work as the chief *qadi* for nine months.

MOORISH KINGDOM

- ☞ Muslims in Spain

When Ibn Battuta returned to Morocco in 1349, he learned that his parents had died. He decided to travel to al-Andalus—the Islamic kingdom of southern Spain—to help defend it from the Christian kingdom in the north. By the time he arrived, the two sides were at peace. Instead, Ibn Battuta visited Valencia and Granada, home of the great Islamic Alhambra Palace (left).

A PILGRIMAGE

- ★ Footprints on the mountain
- ★ But whose feet?

Ibn Battuta visited Sri Lanka to make a pilgrimage to a **sacred** mountain called Adam's Peak. At the top, the rock formation is indented with what looks like a huge footprint. Buddhists say it is a footprint of Buddha. Hindus believe it belongs to the god Shiva. Muslims see it as the footprint of Adam, the first human and first prophet.

IBN BATTUTA'S TRAVELS IN DAR AL-ISLAM

Ibn Battuta's journeys took him across much of Asia and northern Africa. The exact route he took is not known for every part of his different travels, but this map shows the path modern scholars believe he took.

New Sarai

Constantinople

ANATOLIA

SPAIN

Granada

Jerusalem

Baghdad

Fez

Cairo

ARABIA

EGYPT

Mecca

AFRICA

Timbuktu

Mogadishu

Granada

Granada was an important city in al-Andalus, an Islamic kingdom set up in southern Spain by Muslims from North Africa in the 700s. Ibn Battuta visited the region in 1350 and toured Muslim cities such as Valencia and Cordóba. In Granada he visited the renowned palace known as the Alhambra.

Key

→ **Journey 1325–1327**

→ **Journey 1327–1341**

→ **Journey 1341–1354**

Modern national borders

Scale

0	1000 miles
0	2000 km

Jerusalem

Ibn Battuta visited Jerusalem in 1326 on a trip to Damascus in Syria. Jerusalem was sacred to Jews, Christians, and Muslims. At the time, it was under the control of the Egyptian Mamluk dynasty.

Delhi

Delhi was the capital of the Delhi Sultanate, a state that covered much of northern India. Although the rulers of the sultanate were Muslims, most of their Indian subjects were Hindus. Ibn Battuta expressed surprise that the two groups of people were able to live among each other and get along well.

Locator map

Hangzhou

Ibn Battuta arrived in China in about 1346. He stayed with an Egyptian family in a neighborhood for Muslim merchants in Hangzhou, which he said was the largest city he had ever seen. The city sat on a large lake, surrounded by gentle green hills.

ASIA

CHINA

Hangzhou

Delhi

INDIA

Pagan

Calicut

Sumatra

N

NE

E

SE

S

SW

W

NW

Mecca

Ibn Battuta visited Mecca in Arabia six times to perform the hajj, or Islamic pilgrimage. Mecca is the site of the Kaaba, the holiest place in Islam. During the hajj, pilgrims walk around the Kaaba seven times. Muslims all over the world are required to face toward the Kaaba when they perform their daily prayers.

Sumatra

The island of Sumatra in Indonesia was the easternmost state to have a Muslim ruler. Islam spread through South and Southeast Asia due to Arabian merchants, who introduced their faith as they traveled.

Meet the Crew

As an educated man, Ibn Battuta was welcomed by sultans and kings. He also visited many centers of learning and met with scholars and religious leaders.

SULTAN OF INDIA
+ A dangerous employer

In India, Ibn Battuta became a judge or *qadi* at the court of Muhammad bin Tughluq, sultan of Delhi (left). The wealthy sultan invited many scholars to his court and spoke many languages, including Persian, Arabic, Turkish, and Sanskrit. But Tughluq was unpredictable and dangerous—he had killed his own father in order to take the throne. Tughluq often treated Ibn Battuta as a trusted advisor, but at other times he suspected him of **treason**. Ibn Battuta feared for his life. After six years, he was eager to escape the sultan's control.

WRITE YOUR MEMOIRS!

- What's the story?
- The sultan wants to know

The only reason we know about Ibn Battuta's travels is thanks to Sultan Abu Inan Faris of Morocco. The sultan lived in the royal palace in Fez (right). When Ibn Battuta returned to Morocco for good in 1354, the sultan encouraged, or possibly ordered, the traveler to write his memoir. A few years later, the sultan was murdered by one of his own advisors.

A CHRISTIAN PRINCESS

☛ **Ibn Battuta accompanies Bayalun**

One of the few women named in the *Rihla* is Princess Bayalun. She was the daughter of the Christian Byzantine emperor and wife of the Muslim sultan Muhammad Öz Beg. Ibn Battuta joined an expedition to escort the pregnant princess to her father's home in Constantinople. It was Ibn Battuta's first visit to Christian lands. He saw the Basilica of Hagia Sophia, or Holy Wisdom. As Ibn Battuta was a Muslim, he did not enter the Christian church, but he met a priest from the **Orthodox** branch of Christianity to discuss a visit to Jerusalem.

My Explorer Journal

★ **Ibn Battuta visited many holy men to ask them about religion. If you wanted to find out about other religions today, who do you think would be best to talk to? Give reasons for your answers.**

> I was amazed at their belief in the merits of one who, though not of their religion, had entered their holy places."
>
> *Ibn Battuta describes the respect with which he was treated by Christian monks because he had visited Jerusalem.*

PAYING RESPECTS

★ **Meeting holy men**

In addition to meeting kings and sultans, Ibn Battuta often made special trips to visit holy men of different faiths. While in Chittagong in modern Bangladesh, Ibn Battuta made a one-month detour to visit Shah Jalal, a Muslim who lived in a cave and had many disciples. He also visited Taoist monks on Mount Qingyuan in eastern China. In Anatolia, he visited the **mausoleum** of Jalal al-Din Rumi (above). Rumi was a follower of **Sufism**. He was also a famous Muslim poet.

Check Out the Ride

Ibn Battuta began his first pilgrimage by riding a donkey alone across North Africa, but he would travel the world in many different ways. In the Middle Ages, nearly everyone traveled mainly on foot.

WILL IT FLOAT?

+ Ibn Battuta distrusts boats

+ Hates sea travel!

Pilgrims heading to Mecca often had to sail across the Red Sea (right). The sea could be dangerous, with coral reefs, rocky shores, and many storms. Ibn Battuta traveled in Arab boats, called *jalbas*. Jalbas were made of wooden slats tied together and covered in grease to make them waterproof. This made their **hull** more flexible than nailed planks, which would break apart if they hit rocks. But the jalbas were often dangerously overcrowded, so they threatened to turn over. Ibn Battuta did not enjoy these trips!

TRAVEL UPDATE

Use Horsepower

☆ Instead of traveling on foot, why not try horsepower? Horses are expensive in North Africa, the Middle East, and Europe, where only the wealthy can afford to use them. On the **steppes** of Central Asia, Ibn Battuta found there were so many horses that they were cheap. Mongol and Turkish **nomads** used horses and oxen to pull wagons or carts loaded with their possessions (left).

THAT'S NOT JUNK!

★ **Chinese ships are huge**

★ **And luxurious**

Ibn Battuta first saw Chinese junks (below right) in Calicut, India. These ocean-going junks were huge sailboats with large oars that each had 10 oarsmen. The ships were so large that they could carry up to 1,000 men and tons of cargo. The Chinese empire had its own fleet of junks, and Chinese merchants used the boats to travel the oceans of Asia. Wealthy passengers could stay in large suites with a private bathroom.

★ **Imagine taking a trip on a bus, in a car, or on an airplane. Now, imagine making that same trip on a camel caravan, covering 20 miles (32 km) a day! Make a list of the kind of things that might be different about the two journeys.**

Did you know ?

Once, after a particularly difficult walk in Oman, Ibn Battuta's feet were so swollen and bloody, he had to rest for days before the pain went away and he could continue.

 Weather Forecast

IN THE DESERT

In Arabia and the Sahara Desert, people traveled in camel caravans. Some camels carried shaded compartments to protect pilgrims from the sun (left). In Africa, caravans traveled only in the early morning and late afternoon. Travelers set up shelter to get out of the midday sun. Arab nomads called Bedouins took sheep with their caravans to produce butter and milk.

Solve It With Science

Ibn Battuta's adventures were possible thanks to a golden age of scholarship and scientific advancement, when scholars were welcomed across Dar al-Islam.

Wisdom

Islamic scholars preserved scientific texts from ancient Greece. The texts covered subjects such as geography, astronomy, and medicine. The West only found out about these texts via the Muslim world.

BUILDING SHIPS

☞ Traditional construction

☞ And triangular sails

The Islamic Golden Age was supported by a growth in maritime trade. This trade was based on ships known as dhows, which traveled the Mediterranean and the Indian Ocean. Like jalbas, dhows are made from planks that are tied together. Dhows have a triangular sail mounted on an angle from the mast. This allows the crew to adjust the sail to catch the wind. Wooden dhows are still built and used today in the region (right).

FINDING THE WAY

★ Measuring latitude

★ With a piece of wood

In order to figure out their position north or south, known as latitude, Arab navigators invented the kamal to help find their way at sea. The kamal is a small piece of wood with a knotted string through a hole in the middle. Sailors put the string in their teeth and held the wood at arm's length. They slid the piece of wood along the string until it blocked Polaris, the North Star. They counted knots to measure the distance from their eye to the piece of wood. That distance allowed them to figure out their rough latitude.

BEAUTIFUL COAL?

+ Ibn Battuta gets it wrong

Porcelain had been invented in China over 2,000 years before Ibn Battuta visited. The Chinese had learned that heating a type of clay to very high temperatures—up to 2,600° Fahrenheit (1,427° Celsius)—produced a glasslike ceramic. Porcelain (right) is much harder than most other ceramics and can seem **translucent**. Ibn Battuta mistakenly reported that it was made from coal!

My Explorer Journal

★ **Ibn Battuta found the world was full of remarkable technology. He tried to describe things for readers who had never seen them. Try writing a description of a modern invention for someone who has never seen it.**

Did you know ?

One way scholars learned about the world was by debate. One person would make an argument, which the other person challenged. In that way, they hoped to discover what was true.

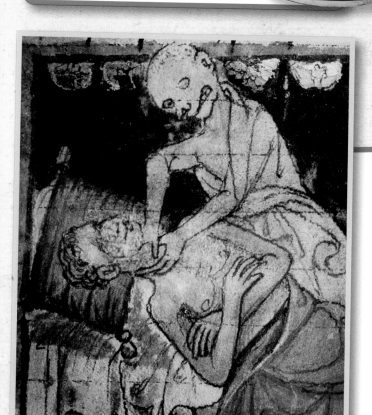

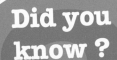

ESCAPING DEATH

☞ **Black Death spreads**

☞ **Ibn Battuta stays ahead**

While Ibn Battuta was traveling home from China, an **epidemic** of **bubonic plague** spread from Central Asia along the Silk Road to Europe. Between 1346 and 1353, the disease killed at least 75 million people. Today we know that plague is transmitted by fleas that live on rats. At the time, people thought God or Allah was punishing them (left). Ibn Battuta was lucky to avoid it. He returned home to learn that his mother had died of the plague in 1349.

Hanging at Home

Ibn Battuta lived in many different places during his travels. Sometimes he lived in luxury, but at other times he lived like a simple pilgrim.

THANK YOU VERY MUCH!

- Traveler receives many gifts
- Including slaves

It was Muslim tradition to give gifts and hospitality to pilgrims and travelers. But Ibn Battuta also impressed people with his learning and his stories of travel. The rulers he visited gave him many gifts, from camels, clothes, and food for his travels to money, jewels, cloth, and slaves, which were common in the Islamic world (above).

TRAVEL UPDATE

Learn While You Stay

★ If you're traveling in Islamic countries, try becoming a student. Ibn Battuta stayed in many madrasas, which are colleges of Islamic studies. Ibn Battuta lived as a scholar, teaching students and discussing Islamic law with other scholars. Madrasas welcomed travelers, so Ibn Battuta stayed in many all over Dar al-Islam.

My Explorer Journal

★ **Ibn Battuta sometimes felt uncomfortable about other cultures. Imagine how it would feel to be in a new place where people lived in a different way. Make a list of the kind of things that might be different.**

FOLLOWING THE RULES

+ Traveler encounters new customs

Ibn Battuta came from a very orthodox Islamic culture, so he was often upset by local customs that disregarded Islamic rules. In Central Asia, he was frustrated that Muslims drank alcohol—even the Sultan got drunk. In Mali, women freely interacted with men outside their family. Locals in the Maldives wore very little clothing. Throughout Dar al-Islam, men often failed to attend Friday prayers even when the **muezzin** called them to prayer (left). Such behavior angered Ibn Battuta.

EATING WHAT'S OFFERED

★ **It's rude to refuse**

★ **Whatever's on your plate**

As an honored guest, Ibn Battuta often ate very well. Good manners required him to eat the food his hosts offered, even if it seemed unusual to him. In North Africa he tried locusts (right), in India he tried tropical fruits and crane meat, and in Central Asia it was horse milk and horse meat.

Meeting and Greeting

Most of the people Ibn Battuta met were Muslim, but they came from a range of different cultures, and many lived in different ways. He also met followers of major religions.

Whirling

One way in which Sufi Muslims tried to communicate with God was by dancing. They spun around rapidly to make themselves light-headed. They were called whirling dervishes.

AN EARLY PROPHECY

- ☞ Ibn Battuta has a dream

- ☞ It later comes true

Early in his travels, Ibn Battuta visited an Egyptian holy man named Abu Abdallah al-Murshidi. By interpreting a dream the traveler had, al-Murshidi said that Ibn Battuta would visit India, stay there for years, and be rescued by an Indian. Ibn Battuta believed the **prophecy** had come true when he was attacked by bandits outside Delhi and rescued by a Muslim villager!

PERSIAN DANCERS

+ Sufis live simple lives

+ Express faith through dance

When Ibn Battuta traveled through Iraq and Persia, he met many Sufi Muslims. The Sufis try to make a direct connection to Allah by using poetry, music, and dance (right). Sufis lived as **ascetics**. This meant they ate only simple foods, did not drink alcohol, and lived simple lives. Ibn Battuta studied the teachings of Sufism. He was interested in the idea of making a **mystical** connection with God.

A CHRISTIAN POPULATION

- Orthodox faith in Anatolia
- Population speaks Greek

While most of Anatolia was ruled by a Muslim sultan, the population were Greek-speaking Christians. Anatolia had been part of the eastern Roman Empire. After the western Roman part of the empire fell in 476 CE, the eastern part survived as the Byzantine Empire. The Byzantines spoke Greek, not Latin, and followed the Orthodox Church. Ibn Battuta found the Orthodox Christians hospitable—and good cooks.

Did you know ?

Christians in the Cappadocia region of Anatolia carved their churches inside formations of soft rock (left). People also made homes inside the rock pillars, which are sometimes called "fairy chimneys."

THE HINDUS

- ★ Majority in India
- ★ Thousands of deities

Muslims from Central Asia had ruled India for over 100 years when Ibn Battuta arrived in 1334. While many Indians converted to Islam, most of the population remained Hindu. Hinduism is the oldest surviving religion in the world. Unlike other religions, it has no founder, no leaders, and no common rituals. There are thousands of **deities** in Hinduism. Different villages and towns focus their worship on unique gods (right).

Far From Home

In the *Rihla*, Ibn Battuta described the Islamic world as being divided between seven mighty leaders. He called them the seven sultans.

Mongols

The Mongols were nomads from Central Asia. In the early 1300s, Genghis Khan founded a vast Mongol Empire. After his death the empire split into different parts. Most later became Muslim states.

SEVEN RULERS

- ☛ Sultans of Islam
- ☛ Rule vast kingdoms

Four of the Islamic leaders were descendants of the Mongol leader Genghis Khan. They ruled over separate parts of what had once been a single empire stretching across Asia from Turkey to China. Then there was the Sultan of Delhi, who controlled most of India. The Sultan of Morocco ruled over Algeria, Tunisia, and Morocco. He and the Sultan of Egypt and Syria controlled much of North Africa and the Middle East.

THE GOLDEN HORDE

- ★ Mongols in Central Asia
- ★ Capital at New Sarai

One of the Mongolian sultans was Muhammed Öz Beg (right, on horse). He was khan, or ruler, of the Golden Horde, a vast territory between the Black Sea and Siberia. The people of the Golden Horde were Turkic and Mongolian nomads who herded animals on the steppes of Central Asia. Ibn Battuta met the Sultan in his capital, New Sarai, on the Volga River in Russia.

EDGE OF DAR AL-ISLAM

- ☛ Into Southeast Asia
- ☛ Visits Sumatra

On his way to China, Ibn Battuta traveled through the Strait of Malacca around the Malay Peninsula. The Malay rulers had welcomed Muslim traders for centuries. By the time Ibn Battuta arrived, many Malays had converted to Islam. The traveler spent two weeks on the island of Sumatra (right) as a guest of the sultan. This was the most eastern kingdom ruled by a Muslim. Today, Sumatra is part of Indonesia, a Muslim country.

TRAVEL UPDATE

Merchant Community

★ If you're a merchant, you may find that cities have special areas for foreign traders. Ibn Battuta lived with other Muslims in Hangzhou in China when he visited in 1346. Most Chinese were Buddhists and Taoists, but they welcomed Muslim merchants because they were eager to make money through trade.

Did you know ?

Ibn Battuta did not really like China. He thought the Chinese were **pagans** who worshiped idols and ancestral spirits. But he did say that China was the safest country for travelers he had visited.

I Love Nature

The *Rihla* describes landscapes, including deserts, grasslands, and mountains. Ibn Battuta came across plants and animals he had never seen before.

First Hippo

In Mali, Ibn Battuta saw his first hippopotamus. Hippos live both on land and in rivers. They eat plants but can be aggressive when threatened. Hippos will attack boats that get too close to them.

IS THAT A UNICORN?

☞ A dangerous animal

IN THE DESERT
★ Special adaptations

Arabian camels, or dromedaries, are adapted to life in the desert (below). Their hump stores up to 80 pounds (36 kg) of fat. The camel uses the fat for nutrition when there is no other food or water. Camels do not sweat, so they do not lose water in high temperatures. They can also close their nostrils to keep out blowing sand, and long eyelashes protect their eyes. Their thick footpads make it easy to walk across both rocks and hot sand.

In India, Ibn Battuta recorded seeing an animal on the banks of the Indus River that was so ferocious it could drive away elephants. He called it a *karkadann* (above). This was a **mythical** creature with a single horn, also known as the Persian unicorn. In fact, what Ibn Battuta had seen was an Indian rhinoceros. A male rhino can run up to 34 miles per hour (55 kmh)—much faster than an elephant!

Weather Forecast

FIND A BAOBAB

The baobab tree (below) can be a life-saver in hot weather. The tree can grow up to 100 feet (30 m) high and 23 feet (7 m) across. Its crown of branches can provide shade for a whole caravan to rest in when the sun is overhead. Desert travelers found rainwater collected in hollowed-out baobab trunks. Ibn Battuta saw baobabs on his trip to Mali in West Africa. He reported seeing a weaver who had set up his loom inside a hollow baobab!

UNIVERSAL FOOD

★ Grains everywhere

Ibn Battuta described eating millet throughout his travels. However, he used "millet" to describe any food made from cereals or grain, such as wheat, barley, oats, or rice. Millet is made by pounding grain into a powder, then boiling it with water or milk. Most people at the time survived on millet, also known as gruel or porridge.

Fortune Hunting

Ibn Battuta did not set out to look for riches. His purpose for traveling was mostly spiritual. He wanted to learn how to become a more faithful Muslim.

A BETTER MUSLIM

☛ An Islamic duty

☛ Six pilgrimages

Ibn Battuta visited Mecca on the hajj six times. However, the hajj is only one of what are known as the Five Pillars of Islam. The others include reciting the **profession of faith**, praying five times a day, and giving money to charity. The final requirement is to fast during the hours of daylight in a special month called Ramadan. Many Muslims get up very early in order to eat a meal while it is still dark (above).

GOING WITHOUT!

+ Living on charity

Like other Islamic pilgrims, Ibn Battuta depended on the third pillar of Islam during his journeys—charitable giving. Providing hospitality to travelers was one type of charity. Muslims gave pilgrims free food, clothes, and shelter along the way. A number of times, Ibn Battuta lost all his possessions due to bandits, pirates, storms, and shipwrecks. At those times, he relied on charity to survive.

TRAVEL UPDATE

Make Yourself Useful

★ Travelers accepting hospitality from their hosts have responsibilities in return. Ibn Battuta, for example, entertained his hosts with stories about the places he had visited. The stories must have sounded wonderful to people who had never traveled far. For his hosts in places such as India and the Maldives, Ibn Battuta also gave them advice about Islamic law.

HERE AND GONE!

★ Ibn Battuta enjoys wealth

★ And abandons it!

As a judge, Ibn Battuta was honored wherever he traveled. Although he sometimes enjoyed a wealthy lifestyle, he often left his belongings behind when it was time to move on (right). It was difficult to move many possessions around when traveling by camel or horse.

SPIRITUAL WEALTH

★ Questioning others

★ Learning about faith

For Ibn Battuta, increasing his understanding of Islam was more important than acquiring wealth. He stayed at madrasas all over Dar al-Islam, and was eager to discuss the Islamic faith. He did not only explore different branches of Islam. He also questioned priests from other religions, such as Orthodox Christianity (left), about their faiths.

This Isn't What It Said in the Brochure!

When Ibn Battuta left Tangier for the first time, he faced many challenges. He suffered from homesickness and cried whenever he thought of his parents. He learned early on how difficult travel could be.

GETTING SICK

★ **Often falls ill**

★ **Comes close to death**

Traveling could be a risky business. Ibn Battuta often became sick. On his very first trip to Mecca, he suffered from fever and diarrhea, but he refused to rest. He was so weak he had to ask his companions to strap him into his saddle so he could continue to ride. Many times he was in danger of dying and had to stay in one place for many months to recover from illness. Ibn Battuta was lucky, however. He noted that some of his traveling companions did die from the same illnesses he had, but he managed to survive.

HAND IT OVER!

+ **Bandits in the desert**

+ **And pirates at sea**

Bandits and pirates were a regular problem for travelers in the Middle Ages. When Ibn Battuta left Delhi, bandits attacked his caravan (above). On a sea voyage about a year later, he was attacked by 12 pirate ships. The pirates boarded Ibn Battuta's ship and took everything he and his companions had, including most of their clothes. The pirates then stranded them on shore and took the ship.

BRR... IT'S COLD

Ibn Battuta sometimes suffered bitterly cold conditions. On the steppes of Central Asia in winter, he wore three coats and two pairs of trousers. His clothes restricted his movement so much he had to be lifted onto his horse. It was so cold that even water he had heated to wash with froze in his beard.

> "The moisture that dripped from my nose would freeze on my moustache."
> *Ibn Battuta on traveling in winter.*

My Explorer Journal

★ **Ibn Battuta felt desperate when the ship sailed away with the Sultan's presents. Imagine you have lost something valuable. Write a letter to your parents explaining how it happened and how it makes you feel.**

Disaster

The Sultan of Delhi asked Ibn Battuta to take valuable gifts to China. But after Ibn Battuta loaded the gifts on a ship, it sailed without him. Afraid to return to Delhi, he decided to head to China anyway!

SHIPWRECK!

☛ Ships often sink

☛ Close escapes for travelers

Ibn Battuta was afraid of traveling by sea—with good reason. Sinkings were common (left). In Calicut, India, he saw the ship he was supposed to sail on destroyed by a storm. Many people died, and all the cargo sank. In Sri Lanka, his ship started to sink. Some of Ibn Battuta's companions escaped on a raft, but he waited all night on the sinking ship to be rescued. He was terrified!

End of the Road

Ibn Battuta returned home to Morocco for good in 1354, 29 years after leaving. He visited Tangier, then moved to Fez, the home of the Sultan of Morocco's court.

A SULTAN'S REQUEST

- Ibn Battuta thinks back
- Dictates his stories

In Fez (above), Sultan Abu Inan Faris wanted Ibn Battuta to record the story of his travels. Working from memory, Ibn Battuta described his experiences to a literary scholar named Ibn Juzayy. The account was published under the title *A Gift to Those who Contemplate Cities and the Marvels of Traveling* in 1355. It soon became known simply as *Rihla*, which means *The Travels*.

TRAVEL UPDATE

Find a Good Helper!

★ If you decide to ask someone to write down a story on your behalf, make sure he or she is reliable. Modern experts know that Ibn Battuta could not have visited all the places he claims at the times he said he was there. Ibn Juzayy is partly to blame. He included descriptions of places, such as Damascus, by other travelers without acknowledging his sources.

Scholar

Ibn Battuta dictated his memoirs to a man named Ibn Juzayy. He came from al-Andalus in southern Spain, and had studied history and law. Ibn Juzayy died only two years after writing *Rihla*.

A RECORD BREAKER

★ **Travels farther than anyone else**

Ibn Battuta was probably the most well-traveled person of the Middle Ages. He traveled through virtually the whole of the Muslim world. He visited famous ancient sites (left) and modern cities. The route he traveled crossed 44 modern countries.

MYSTERIOUS ENDING

☛ Ibn Battuta fades from view

☛ No records of his death

After spending most of his life traveling, Ibn Battuta settled down as a judge in his native Morocco (right). There are no records about his life after his travels. Historians are not even sure when he died, but it was probably around 1368 or 1369.

GLOSSARY

ambassador An official who represents a ruler or country abroad

ascetics People who live acccording to strict rules, with no form of luxury or enjoyment

bubonic plague A deadly disease transmitted by fleas carried on rats

caravan A group of people and animals traveling together

deities Gods and goddesses

epidemic A widespread outbreak of disease

hull The main body of a ship or boat

Islam A religious faith founded in Arabia in the 600s by Muhammad

mausoleum An impressive building holding a tomb or tombs

muezzin A man who calls Muslims to pray from a tower called a minaret

mystical Inspiring a sense of spiritual mystery

mythical Occurring in stories and folk tales

nomads People who move around to live, with no permanent home

Orthodox A branch of Christianity based in Eastern Europe and Greece

pagans People with religious beliefs different from the main world religions

pilgrimage A journey made to a holy place for a religious reason

profession of faith A declaration that a particular religion is the one true religion

prophecy A prediction of something that will happen in the future

sacred Extremely holy and worthy of respect

sharia Islamic law based on the Koran and the teachings of the Prophet Muhammad

steppes Large areas of grassland in eastern Europe and Central Asia

sultan A Muslim ruler

Sufism A Muslim spiritual or belief system where followers can achieve a mystical union with God

Sunni A follower of the largest branch of the Islamic faith. Followers of the other main branch are called the Shia

treason The crime of betraying one's country

translucent Allows light through but not clearly seen through

Ibn Battuta is born to a Berber family in Tangier, in what is now Morocco.

Ibn Battuta visits Mecca in Saudi Arabia to make the first of six visits to the hajj, or Islamic pilgrimage.

After another hajj in Mecca, Ibn Battuta visits Asia Minor (modern-day Turkey), where he meets Byzantine Christians.

Ibn Battuta leaves India after losing gifts from the Sultan of Delhi intended for the rulers of China. He visits Ceylon (Sri Lanka).

1304 **1325** **1326** **1327** **1328** **1332** **1341**

Ibn Battuta leaves home on his travels and heads toward Egypt on his way to Arabia.

Ibn Battuta travels to the east coast of Africa and visits the Persian Gulf.

Ibn Battuta arrives in India, where he becomes an Islamic judge in the service of the Sultan of Delhi.

ON THE WEB

www.quatr.us/africa/literature/ibnbattuta.htm
A biography of Ibn Battuta written for kids by Professor Karen Carr of Portland State University.

www.orias.berkeley.edu/resources-teachers/travels-ibn-battuta
The introductory page to an extensive site about Ibn Battuta and his travels, with maps of his journey and quotations from the *Rihla*.

www.alchemistconnector.weebly.com/timeline-of-ibn-battuta.html
A timline of Ibn Battuta's life and travels.

https://school.bighistoryproject.com/media/khan/articles/U8_Battuta_2014_890L.pdf
An illustrated downloadable booklet about Ibn Battuta from Big History Project.

BOOKS

Harmon, Daniel E. *Ibn Battuta: The Medieval World's Greatest Traveler* (The Silk Road's Greatest Travelers). Rosen Young Adult, 2016.

Sharafeddine, Fatima. *The Amazing Travels of Ibn Battuta*. Groundwood Books, 2014.

Toth, Henrietta. *Ibn Battuta: The Greatest Traveler of the Muslim World* (Spotlight on Explorers and Colonization). Rosen Publishing Group, 2017.

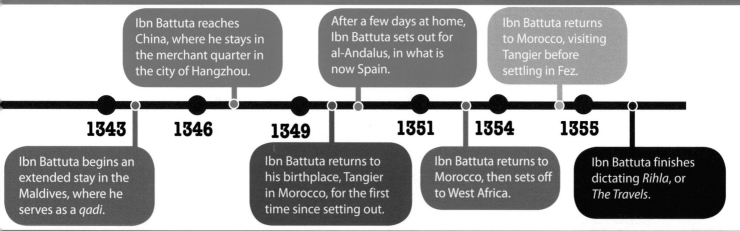

1343 Ibn Battuta begins an extended stay in the Maldives, where he serves as a *qadi*.

Ibn Battuta reaches China, where he stays in the merchant quarter in the city of Hangzhou.

1346

1349 Ibn Battuta returns to his birthplace, Tangier in Morocco, for the first time since setting out.

After a few days at home, Ibn Battuta sets out for al-Andalus, in what is now Spain.

1351

1354 Ibn Battuta returns to Morocco, then sets off to West Africa.

Ibn Battuta returns to Morocco, visiting Tangier before settling in Fez.

1355 Ibn Battuta finishes dictating *Rihla*, or *The Travels*.

INDEX

A

Abu Inan Faris, Sultan 10, 28

al-Andalus 7, 8

Anatolia 11, 19

B

Bangladesh 11

baobab tree 23

Bayalun, Princess 11

Bedouin 13

Berbers 4

bubonic plague 15

C

camels 13, 22, 25

Central Asia 6, 12, 15, 17, 19, 20, 27

China 6, 9, 11, 15, 21, 27

Christianity 7, 11, 19, 25

Constantinople 11

D

Dar al-Islam 6, 8–9, 17, 25

Delhi 9, 10, 20, 26, 27

deserts 13, 22

F

Fez 10, 28

Five Pillars of Islam 24

food 17, 23

G

Genghis Khan 20

Golden Horde 20

H

hajj 5, 9, 24

Hinduism 7, 9, 19

hippopotamuses 22

horses 12, 25

hospitality 16, 24, 25

Hangzhou 9, 21

I

Ibn Juzayy 28, 29

India 6, 10, 13, 18, 19, 22

Indonesia 9, 21

Islam 4, 5, 6, 9, 19, 21, 25

Islamic law 5, 7, 17, 25

J L

Jerusalem 8

languages 5, 10

M

madrasas 16

Malacca, Strait of 21

Maldives 7, 17

Mali 17, 22, 23

map 8–9

Mecca 5, 9, 12, 24

Mongols 6, 12, 20

Morocco 4, 7, 10, 22, 28, 29

Muhammad 5, 24

Muhammad Öz Beg 11, 20

My Explorer Journal 11, 13, 15, 17, 23, 27, 29

N O P

navigation 14

Orthodox Church 19, 25

pilgrimage 5, 9, 12

porcelain 15

R

Ramadan 24

Red Sea 12

rhinoceros 22

Rihla 4, 10, 11, 16, 28

Rumi 11

S

scholarship 14, 15, 29

sharia *see* Islamic law

shipping 12, 13, 14, 27

Silk Road 6, 15

slaves 16

Spain 7, 8

Sri Lanka 7

Sufis 11, 18

Sumatra 9, 21

T W

Tangier 4,26, 28

Trabiz 6

trade 14, 21

transportation 12–13, 22, 27

Travels *see Rihla*

Travel Update 6, 12, 16, 21, 25

Tughluq, Muhammad bin 10

Weather Forecast 13, 27